Te

Gemma Hooper

Telling tales © 2022 Gemma Hooper

All rights reserved.

No part of this publication may be reproduced, stored in a retrieval system, or transmitted, in any form or by any means, electronic, mechanical, photocopying, recording or otherwise, without the prior written permission of the presenters.

Gemma Hooper asserts the moral right to be identified as author of this work.

Presentation by *BookLeaf Publishing*

Web: www.bookleafpub.com

E-mail: info@bookleafpub.com

ISBN: 978-93-95755-60-3

First edition 2022

For Mum who always knew that I was a poet at heart.

For my beautiful, funny and caring family who provide endless love and support.

ACKNOWLEDGEMENT

Thank you to all of the wonderful children and adults that I have had the great privilege to work with who have inspired many of my poems.

The common sense shop

Have you seen the common sense shop?
It's mentioned every day.
I'm supposed to go before school,
But I don't know the way!
Isabelle, she seems to know,
She nods along and smiles,
Where is this common sense shop?
It better not be miles!
I'll be sure to find it later,
Miss says to take a friend,
I'll find the common sense shop,
I'll get there in the end!

Glue sticks

The year began with plenty,
We even had our own,
By half term we were sharing,
Miss began to groan,
By Christmas we were down to ten,
It was tricky making cards,
I used the last of mine on glitter,
For the Bethlehem bright star.
By Easter we had only six,
The PVA was out,
Miss commenced the panic,
She began to ask about.
Each teacher had the same old tale,
They had run out too!
TAs were on a mission to find a hiding glue.
At summer we were down to one,
Miss kept it in her drawer,
As an end-of-year leaving gift,
I gave Miss 30 more!

The great escape

My teacher has a hamster,
He's cute and brown and white,
He sleeps all day through lessons,
And wakes up in the night.
He buries himself in papery shred,
Curls tight into a ball.
In the daytime we just wouldn't know,
He's really there at all!
One morning, looking worried,
Our teacher searched around,
She sighed and told us sadly,
That he could not be found!
We searched and called his name for the first
part of the day,
We did not expect to find him in the dinner hall
at play!
He had had a fine old time,
He'd made friends with the cook.
Next time that he goes missing,
We'll know exactly where to look.

Seagull attack

Running through the playground in my mufti orange top,
Seagulls chasing after me,
Not just one-a flock!
A gang had been waiting for the moment to attack,
I had been a target with my tiger-themed backpack!
My teachers didn't notice that I had whizzed straight past,
I sped around the school with them flying very fast.
Now I don't like gulls,
They gave me quite a fright.
I won't forget that day,
The day the gulls took flight!

There's an apple in the toilet!

Miss, there's an apple in the toilet,
There's a leak in the sink,
There's a spider in the cloakroom,
There's an eyelash in my blink.

There's a graze on my knee,
There's a bump on my head,
There's a letter in my bookbag,
No PE on my peg!

Miss, I've got permission slips,
Miss, can you change my book?
Miss, I've got a broken pencil.
Miss, I've lost 20p for tuck.

Miss, I've done my work,
Miss, I've passed my test,
Miss, I've learnt a lot this year,
Miss, you are the best!

Bearly a camel

My one and only line was to roar,
Roar like a bear they said.
I had to jump from behind the piano,
Dressed as a camel instead!

Long division song

First you take the divisor,
Multiples set out,
Yes-you get the multiple and you lay them out,
Now you get the nearest one,
How many will fit?
Place the quotient on the top-check that it fits!
Subtract the multiple down below,
Work out the difference then go...
Then you got to bring it down;
Bring the digit down,
And repeat again,
Just keep going!
We're gonna be division kings!
I just love division!

Diary of a lemon

When mum asked me about my day at school,
I recalled my writing challenge:

Today I feel bitter,
Today I am mellow,
Today I am sour,
Today I am yellow.
Today I am zesty,
Today I am zing,
Today I am sharp,
Today I am ting.

Mum wasn't so sure on theme I'd been set,
"I think your teacher said: DILEMAS instead!"
Oops, I'll confess my confusion,
I'll own up right away,
When she's marking my work,
"What a lemon!" she'll say.

Stop swinging on your chair Sam

"Stop swinging on that chair Sam,
You'll fall, you'll crash, you'll sway.
Stop swinging on your chair Sam,
We tell you every day!
Stop swinging on your chair Sam,
It's going to break or crack!
Stop swinging on your chair Sam,
You'll fall and hurt your back!
Stop swinging on your chair Sam,
You'll have to stand instead.
Stop swinging on your chair Sam,
You'll fall and bump your head!"

After breaktime Sam arrived to find,
His chair had shrank to infant size!

"Stop swinging on your chair Sam,
The legs will come right off!
Stop swinging on your chair Sam,
Your chair has had enough!"

By lunchtime, Sam's chair had shrank once more,
His doll-sized chair now on the floor!

Beware all the children that like to sway.
Your chair might shrink like Sam's one day!

Lost property

It happened... and it happened to ME!
I'd seen them before swimming,
I locked them in locker number three!
When we came to get dry,
As my class were waiting for the bus,
My trousers had gone missing,
Miss was calling, "What's the fuss?"
I shouted that my class could go without me as I wasn't going home,
"I'm not going without trousers!
I'd never live it down!"
Miss asked among the lifeguards,
They rummaged in the box,
I wore someone else's trousers home,
They smelled of lost property old socks!

Sue

The brightest smile and warmest heart was
owned by our TA,
Her laugh ricocheted around the classroom,
She brought sunshine to our day.
She always made it simpler,
With her it all made sense,
Thank you Miss for your care,
And the time with us you spent.
We'll miss you every day,
We're sad we had to part,
You'll always be here with us,
Carried in our hearts.

My Grandad is a butterfly

Grandad is now an orange butterfly,
He grew wings and flew away,
I feel him near when Spring has sprung,
With tulip buds in May.
He is now free to fly among the birds, the clouds and bees,
His delicate orange wings now flutter in the breeze.
Back to nature, among the trees,
With him the season grows,
My Grandad is now an orange butterfly,
In heaven's garden-perched on his orange rose.

Brave Katie

She stood in total stillness as it balanced on her nose,
Around her was a frenzy; a riot had arose,
Katie did not mind the wasp,
Katie did not worry.
She didn't swat or flap,
She wasn't in a hurry!
Calmly humming to herself,
She waited for the wasp to go,
She's the bravest in our class,
The bravest person that I know!

The wasp flew off and onto me,
I screamed and ran off fast!
"It's on me! Help me, save me!"
"Are you sure that you're our teacher?"
Little Katie asked.

Year six

Ring the bell,
Set up the hall,
Take the registers,
Carry the ball,
Tidy the library,
Answer the phone,
Sit on the benches,
Allowed to walk home!
Lead the prayers,
Help with the tech,
Jobs to do;
Lists to check!
Messages to take,
Resources to get,
Follow my lead,
Example to set,
Help the teachers,
Captain the team,
Read with a buddy,
Year 6 is a dream!

Fraction ballet

My teacher does fraction ballet,
She loves to dance around,
When adding numerators together,
She leaps up off the ground.
She plies for denominators,
Stoops low and points her toes,
She pirouettes around the room,
Chanting factors that she knows.
We watch her in astonishment,
She claps as our multiples we say,
I still can not add fractions,
But I'm better at ballet!

Just a little bit!

"Did you push him?"
"No! It wasn't me!"
"Did you push him a little bit?"
"Just a little you see!"

"Did you kick her?"
"No, I didn't do it!"
"Did you kick her a little bit?"
"Just a little old kick, hardly anything to it!"

"Did you take it?"
"No, I'm not to blame?"
"Did you take some?"
"Just the smallest of smallest of smallest of them!"

"Did you say it?"
"No! I didn't say a thing!"
"Did you say it in a whisper?"
"I thought it and whispered the words on the wind!"

Animal themes

I mentioned ONCE that I like llamas,
Now they're on my bedroom wall!
I have curtains, bedding, pictures,
Llamas on them all!

I once told Dad that I thought dolphins...
Were majestic and quite cool,
Now every gift is dolphin-themed:
Mugs, bags and a pencil case for school!

I was quite partial to giraffes;
So elegant and tall,
Now I have pillows, cups and miniatures,
With giraffes on them all!

Tigers are the theme for me,
I have a tiger room!
Dad's bought: tiger plates, salt and pepper pots,
Even tiger spoons!

Why is it when you say you like an animal
parents go so over the top?
I once said I like Koalas and now my room is
like the zoo shop!

Wet paper towel

Fell and bumped you knee,
Leave it to me!

Paper towel-make it wet,
I'll sort that knee-don't you fret!

Tripped and grazed your arm?
My paper towel will sooth that harm!

Ran too fast and have a scraper,
Pass me towels made from paper!

In a bustle, in a clash,
For paper towels I will dash!

In a wobble, In a mess,
Paper towels I will press!